Gösta Clemens Peter

MÜNSTER
AT ITS BEST

The Sightseeing Book

2nd Edition

Translation by Douglas Brian McTague and Martje Saljé

münstermitte
medienverlag

Contents

Preliminary remarks from the author

As the first edition of my book went out of print, I was incredibly happy to undertake a new edition. After all, because there are many ways to experience a city, there are new impressive motifs to discover. And as inevitable the force of change is, Münster changes too. Many cities carelessly place new buildings wherever without showing much consideration for the past. Yet in Münster, modern buildings are carefully incorporated within the historical fabric, which provides an attractive balance between tradition and modernity. And it is exactly this desire to preserve this balance which makes Münster unique.

Münster – university city, city of churches, city of science, civil servant & student city, episcopal city, city of art and culture, city of the Anabaptist Movement, birthplace of the Peace of Westphalia, bicycle capital . . . and most livable city. In the recent past as well as throughout the centuries Münster has been given numerous titles and hallmarks, admiration and praise, yet also its share of criticisms, for example:

elegant and classy | impressive and steeped in tradition | stubborn and conservative | historical and picturesque | alive and friendly | provincial and expensive | lovably old and excitingly young | home of rain | city of eternal bell ringing | the most beautiful among Germany's beautiful cities.

Nevertheless the beautiful attributes outweigh the criticisms by far. After all, there have been good reasons indeed for honouring Münster as the world's most livable city in 2004 and North Rhine-Westphalia's most beautiful city in 2011. Quiet recently in 2015 the Historical Town Hall, one of our most beautiful buildings, was awarded the European Heritage Label.

I hope that my photo series, which capture various colorful scenes in Münster, can provide you the look, the feel, and the atmosphere that make our city so wonderfully unique and worth living in.

Gösta Clemens Peter
An enthusiastic Münsteran

Gabled Houses, Archways & Boutiques

The Prinzipalmarkt – Münster's Parlour

Where else is there a city with a public space like the Prinzipalmarkt? Münster's parlour is a piece of living urban history. The arcades, once used by women to market their fruits and vegetables, today house upscale shops offering opportunities for window or actual shopping, rain or shine.

The magnificent gabled houses lining both sides of the Prinzipalmarkt take you on a journey to the past. However, these gabled houses are not as old as they look, which has led some critics to deride the Prinzipalmarkt as simply a movie set of Hollywood proportions. During World War II, 91% of the historical downtown was destroyed, of which the Prinzipalmarkt was not spared. Initially, rebuilding the Prinzipalmarkt from the rubble seemed impossible. Then there was the question of just exactly how? Would it be easier to just erect some modern buildings in their place? Eventually the city council decided to rebuild the Prinzipalmarkt and its characteristic gabled houses faithful to its medieval origins, form, and layout. Neighbouring cities, which were also heavily bombed, ridiculed Münster for living up to its Westphalian stubbornness and clinging to an idealised past. These same cities chose to erase their past and rebuild their inner cities accommodating not Germany's cultural and architectural history, nor making space for pedestrians, nor creating human scaled environments, but rather accommodating mainly skyscrapers and cars.

PETZHOLD

Early morning – Prinzipalmarkt

The Prinzipalmarkt is framed on its north side by the steeple of St. Lamberti Church and on its south side by the gleaming green tower of the Town Hall. From end to end 48 three-storey gabled houses, some exhibiting more splendour than others, line each side of the Prinzipalmarkt. These houses, standing shoulder to shoulder, make up the characteristic "zigzag line" look of the Prinzipalmarkt, which can also be seen in the logos of some of the shops. Many events take place in front of this historical curtain backdrop: Heads of State as well as royalty receive the red carpet treatment. Citizens exercise their right to protest. The prince of carnival yearly greets the carnival revellers. Shooting associations march through festively as well as religious processions. Then there are the sporting events such as the bicycle race Münsterland-Giro and the Münster Marathon.

Town Hall tower 1

2 Gabled houses

The love of a good stroll under the arcades are not reserved only for Münsterans. Münster's numerous tourists can experience the Prinzipalmarkt in the summer as it is magnificently adorned with hanging potted Geraniums. Taking the flowers' place in the fall are colourful lanterns, followed by Advent wreaths during the Christmas season, which are lit and illuminate the arcades.

Under the arcades 3

Naturally, the most beautiful gabled house on the Prinzipalmarkt is the Town Hall, which was rebuilt in 1956 nearly true to its original 14th century gothic style. In this building Münster made history. Its former council hall, the so-called "Hall of Peace", served as the site of negotiations for the Peace of Westphalia (1643–1648). In honour of this, the city has left the council chamber in the same condition, in which the peace ambassadors have left it. This was also made possible by the city's wise decision to relocate the chamber's contents during World War II.

Gable of the Historic Town Hall with the flag of the city

Busts of the Anabaptists at the columns of the Town Hall 1

2 Hall of Peace: portraits of the negotiators of the Peace of Westphalia

Historic Town Hall 3

The European Union has also recognised the historical Town Hall and its role as the site of the Peace of Westphalia and as a milestone towards the development of modern Europe. In April 2015, it honoured the Town Hall with the European Heritage Label.

Historic town Hall and "Stadtweinhaus"

The "Stadtweinhaus", which is located right next to the Town Hall, once housed the city scales and wine stores, and the supplies of wine with the city council's monopoly. From the protruding balcony called the "Sentenzbogen", death sentences (then titled "sententia") were once read aloud to the public. Today, however, the "Sentenzbogen" is used for more cheerful occasions.

Christmassy Prinzipalmarkt 1

2 "Hansemahl" open air meal on the "Prinzipalmarkt"

3 Well at St. Lamberti church in front of the gabled houses

Bicycle Highways, Bicycle Garage & Bicycle Wash Bicycle Capital Münster

Adam Opel, founder of the car company Opel, once said that there is no other invention in which usefulness and pleasure are so intimately combined than with the bicycle.

And this is exactly what the citizens of Münster must be thinking when they are on their bikes throughout the city: by sun, wind, or rain. In Münster, everyone rides a bicycle, also named "Leeze". You will see students, men in suits, women in dresses, nuns and clergy, and the police, all on bikes. Being the most popular mode of transportation, it is not surprising that more than 100,000 people commute by bike daily. After all, Münster has a bike path network stretching more than 300 km with special bike related offers. These include designated bike lanes, separate bike traffic signals, as well as the freedom to bike in both directions on many one way streets.

There is also the car-free bicycle highway in the shape of a green belt surrounding the historical city centre, the so-called promenade, which provides access to all parts of the inner city faster than by car. Here bicyclists are given the green light.

schnitzler
viehoff
ARKADE
HAUS MONHOF
schnitzler
Zumnorde
SIGNORA

Bicycles in front of the Diocesan Library

In Münster there are twice as many bicycles as inhabitants. To be exact, there are 2.3 bicycles to each inhabitant. The reason for this is simple: Many Münsterans are dependent on the bicycle as a main mode of transport. Should it no longer work or is left parked in front of one of Münster's numerous Pubs in the Kuhviertel due to excessive drinking, there must always be a second bicycle waiting at home. This also means that Münsterans have various kinds of bicycles: one, most often of lower quality, for everyday use, and the second for serious riding or long tours. Making up the 0.3 in the statistic are bicycles of such low quality that it's no tragedy if they were stolen after they have been left outside for weeks.

With so many bicycles, roughly 6,000 are reported stolen each year. However, the branch of the police specialising in bicycle thefts estimate a much higher figure.

Parked bicycles along the “Promenade” 1

2 Bicyclists on the frozen Lake Aa

The “Promenade” 3

Bicycle garage at the main station

It is also not surprising that Münster, with these many bicycles, is home of Germany's largest bicycle garage with more than 3,500 spaces, even equipped with a bicycle wash.

The sheer number of bicycles around the train station, of which most are properly and orderly parked, nevertheless gives the impression of absolute chaos. Yet it is exactly this chaos of parked bikes which forms and therefore belongs to the city's image.

For its efforts at promoting bicycle use Münster has been recognized with several awards and today is considered a model of bicycle infrastructure for many cities within Germany and abroad.

1 Even the mayor of Münster Markus Lewe goes by bicycle

2 Bicyclists on the "Promenade"

For visitors: If you want the true Münster experience, you absolutely need to hop on a bicycle.

Faith, Hope, Trust

City of Churches

Churches, particularly those with steeples visible from afar, characterise the cityscape. With over 60 of them, it seems only appropriate that Münster is known as "Rome of the north".

Accompanying the churches are the numerous religious orders such as the Franciscans, Clarists, Capuchins, and the Alexians. These, among others, are the core of the religious life in the episcopal city.

As a result the citizens of Münster are often described as rather pious, but that's ultimately a matter of opinion. However, what is remarkable is the fact that within only five years (2001–2005) three figures from Münster and its surrounding regions were beatified: first in 2001 the Clemens sister Maria Euthymia (1914–1955), then in 2004 the mystic Anna Katharina Emmerick (1774–1824), and most recently in 2005 the cardinal of Münster Clemens August Graf von Galen (1878–1946).

1 The steeples of the cathedral at sunset

Astronomical clock 2

St. Paul's Cathedral – the historical origin of the city

Towering right in the heart of the historical city and erected on top of the Horsteberg is St. Paul's Cathedral, which also serves as the center of the bishopric of Münster. The city's beginnings can be traced back to the building of the first Cathedral in 805, which was built during the reign of the first bishop of Münster, Liudger. Today's Cathedral with its prominent steeples is praised as a work of art. Inside the Cathedral you find an astronomical clock, which is not only a technical but an actual work of art as well. The clock, whose calendar reaches into the year 2071, is adorned with chimes and a procession of the Three Holy Kings.

Close to the clock is the Ludgerus Chapel, which is the resting place of Münster's Cardinal Clemens August Graf von Galen (1878–1946), also known as the "Lion of Münster". Risking death, he challenged and preached against the national socialist regime during World War II.

1 St. Lamberti's Church

Watchman Martje Saljé 2

Three wrought-iron cages 3

St. Lamberti – church steeple with a watchman and three cages

The market and town church St. Lamberti, built between 1375 and 1450, is located at the intersection of Münster's oldest trade routes.

At the top of the steeple is Münster's loftiest "office", where the first female watchman carries out her duty. Between 9 pm and midnight you can hear the hooting of her horn every half hour. In Münster, tradition means a great deal. Even though the watchman no longer warns the city of approaching enemy troops, her direct predecessors were active in detecting fires even before the firebrigade were aware.

Though perhaps what St. Lamberti is most famous for is its role in the violent and bloody Anabaptist Movement. The three wrought-iron cages affixed to the steeple high above once contained the tortured and mutilated corpses of the leaders of the failed Anabaptist Movement in the mid-16th century.

Liebfrauen-Überwasser – beheaded yet impressive

The peculiar name of the church is derived from its original name "Santa Maria trans aquas" and is the oldest St. Mary's Church of the Bishopric. The term "trans aquas" (across the waters) is a reference to the fact that the church is situated across the little river Aa from St. Paul's Cathedral.

The prominent and almost quadratic steeple of the church, which, after the Cathedral, is the second oldest church in the historical city centre, was "decapitated" twice. The first time occurred during the Anabaptist Movement, where the top of the steeple was toppled to the ground, in order to make room for cannons. The second "decapitation" in 1704 was caused by a powerful storm, which literally blew off the top. Since then and due to financial reasons, no efforts have been made to refit the steeple with a top.

Church of "Liebfrauen-Überwasser"

Pulpit 2

Gallery

St. Clemens' Church – Schlaun's Gem

St. Clemens' Church was built by the famous Westphalian baroque architect Johann Conrad Schlaun (1695–1773) to serve as the house church to the St. Clemens' Hospital. Today, with its unusual six sided layout, it's arguably the most beautiful and renowned baroque church in Northwest Germany. Its interior is just as beautiful and impressive as the facades.

St. Clemens' Church 3

St. Ludgeri Church

St. Ludgeri Church – unconventional but appealing

With its three steeples St. Ludgeri Church appears striking. Essentially the church was constructed in the Romanesque style, only to expand soon after with the addition of a choir in the Gothic style. Its towers are also dissimilar. The "crowned" crossing tower is probably the most beautiful among Münster's skyline of steeples.

St. Martini Church – varied history with different architectural styles

The St. Martini Church is the first youth church in the diocese of Münster. Originally built as a Romanesque basilica, the church was "modernised" in the 14th century and rebuilt into a three-aisled gothic hall church. Like the Überwasser Church, St. Martini's steeple was toppled during the Anabaptist Movement. Yet unlike Überwasser, it did not fall victim a second time to storm force winds, but to fire during the Seven Years' War. Today the steeple exhibits a rather elegant form, its fourth floor rich in figures of saints.

1 St. Martini Church

2 Apostle Church

Apostle Church – the steeple-less among the pretty churches

The Apostle Church, which is the oldest Minorite's Church in Westphalia and today the main Protestant church of the city, was built in the second half of the 13th century. The fact that is has no steeple is the result of the mendicant monastic order.

Church of the Holy Cross – landmark of a city district

Compared to the other churches, the neo-Gothic Church of the Holy Cross was built rather recently between the years 1898 and 1902. Its steeple is five storeys high (87 m) and towers above the district "Kreuzviertel", thus characterising the look of the basilica. The basilica itself has the layout of a cross with a star shaped crossing where the nave and transept meet.

1 Church of the Holy Cross

Petri Church 2

Petri Church – university and wedding church

The catholic St. Petri Church was built between 1590 and 1597 as a church for the Münster based Jesuit College. Stylistically it stands between gothic and renaissance. During World War II it was almost completely destroyed but rebuilt in its original condition. Today it serves mainly as the church for catholic students, the catholic university community, and it is a popular choice for weddings.

Servatii Church – a place of silence

The Servatii Church is the smallest medieval church in Münster and one of the oldest (built in 1230). Because the church still stands on its original medieval ground level, it appears to have subsided a little when compared to the surrounding buildings.

1 Servatii Church

2 Domenican Church

Dominican Church – baroque church with extraordinary acoustics

With its baroque cupola and its southern European crested steeples, the Dominican Church is a building you would expect to encounter more likely in Southern Europe instead of Westphalia. The contrast in construction materials, with sandstone from the nearby hills named Baumberge used for the facade and red bricks for the walls on both sides is also striking. The rather reserved decor inside combined with the extraordinary acoustics often used for academic music programmes is something peculiar, too.

Students & Professors, Researchers & Thinkers University City Münster

The stately City Palace was originally constructed as a prince-bishop's residence by Johann Conrad Schlaun (1695–1773) and, after his death, later finished by Wilhelm Ferdinand Lipper (1733–1800) from 1767 to 1787. Since 1954 it serves as the official office of the university.

Because the City Palace houses the university's administration and chancellor's' office, there aren't many lecture halls and therefore not many students to be found. The university, which was established in 1780 by the prince-bishop minister and vicar general Franz Freiherr von Fürstenberg (1792–1810), is spread throughout the city. Law and business students, for example, have courses in the inner city, while psychology students reside primarily on the city limits.

Over 50,000 people study and work at the university, with more than 120 departments and 250 buildings for its students, professors, and researchers. As a result, Westphalian Wilhelms-University, in addition to the University of Applied Sciences and its administration, characterise the city scene and life in Münster. You can see this vividly each weekday morning via the heavy bicycle traffic.

The Westphalian Wilhelms-University, which is named after Kaiser Wilhelm II, ranks as one of the largest in Germany. The university is not only the greatest contributor to the city's image, but is also the largest employer together with the University Hospital.

Münster has a tradition of higher education and its medical faculty is renowned within Germany. Over 130 professors and a further 1,000 scholars are spread out over 70 clinics and polyclinics. It's not surprising that Münster has been called "City of Health". The University Hospital's conspicuous 62 m high towers for recovering patients has long become a landmark of the city.

One of the best examples for the university's elite level of research are the associations Cluster of Excellence "Religion and Politics" as well as Cells in Motion. Also among the elite research programs are the Centre for Interdisciplinary Biological Sciences and the State Competence Center for Information, Telecommunication, and Media Law. The city is not only very beautiful but also very intelligent.

Towers of the University Hospital

Academy of Music 1

2 Law school

At the Westphalian Wilhelms-University of Münster the Academy of Music teaches a traditional cultivation of music up to the various forms of modern music. Approximately 300 students from across the globe are taught, accompanied, and supported by nearly 150 teachers.

View into a lecture room 3

In 1973, the opening of the modern library, which is stocked with over 6 million works of academic literature, serves not only as the university library but the state library of Westphalia as well. The facade of the library is adorned with fourteen 2 m large red illuminated letters, spelling out "GEHORCHE KEINEM" (OBEY NO ONE), which triggered a nationwide discussion. The sign designed by the artist Babak Saed and a gift from the Office of the Prime Minister in Düsseldorf, often was wrongly interpreted as an open call to anarchy and not as a plea to the using of information with a critical mind.

University and State Library

The University of Applied Sciences together with roughly 13,900 students spread across twelve departments and two central scientific units is one of the largest technical universities in Germany. Its main offices are located in the picturesque Hüffer Foundation on the street "Hüfferstraße" close to the City Palace.

1 Hüffer Foundation

University canteen at the Lake Aa 2

And as many are aware, studying and working stimulates the appetite. Addressing this are two large university canteens as well as several smaller ones, where not only students and employees can dine, but the general public as well. The largest one, "Mensa am Ring", while conveniently located between many faculties, cannot compete with the beautiful scenery offered by the "Mensa am Aasee". The canteens, which are jokingly referred to as a "fancy-shmancy restaurants", nevertheless offer an impressive range of dishes, stews, salad buffets, desserts, as well as wok dishes – and all at very affordable prices.

"The education of the people is at all times the most important duty of the state." These words were uttered by the university's founder Freiherr Franz von Fürstenberg (1729–1810). His statue can be found at the Domplatz next to the main entrance of the university building, named Fürstenberghaus. Occasionally his sash changes colors whenever a fraternity manages to express their artistic side during the night.

3 Statue of the founder of the university

Lake Aa, Canal, Harbour & more

City of Water

Münster may not be able to compete with the amount of water flowing through Hamburg, but with the Lake Aa, the canal, the harbour, streams, and of course, the water that rains down from above – there is a good deal of water flowing through the city.

Starting with the Lake Aa, it serves as a popular relaxing spot for Münsters citizens in the middle of the city and offers opportunities for sailing, hopping on a pedalo, and if it's cold enough, ice skating as well. The Lake Aa is artificially made with its source, the Aa, flowing from the nearby Baumberge. The lake's water area covers roughly 40 ha and its length spans 2,100 m and thus is popular for runners and walkers alike. Popular attractions such as the All-Weather Zoo and the Mühlenhof Open Air Museum can be comfortably reached by boat aboard the aquabus SOLAARIS, an aluminum catamaran fitted with modern solar technology.

ANTENNE
MÜNSTER

1 Terraces at the Lake Aa

2 Lake Aa in the evening sun

At the banks of the Lake Aa there is plenty to like: enjoying a cup of coffee with a piece of cake, licking an ice cream cone, having a fine dining experience or simply eating currywurst. There is also a sailing school with pedalos to rent. In summer, the Lake Aa is definitely not a place reserved only for citizens.

Right in the neighbourhood of the Lake Aa an oasis for elephants is situated. Their bathing pool in the Elephant Park of the All-Weather Zoo contains an amazing 585 cbm of water and a depth of 2.6 m is enough for even elephants to dive under. Who wouldn't want to be an elephant there!

1 Bathing pleasure for elephants

2 The Aa stream in the city

After flowing through the Lake Aa, the Aa stream continues across the city and the promenade, dividing the historical centre almost in half. The path running along the Aa offers a relaxing break from the hustle and bustle of the city centre.

A larger body of water flowing through the city is the impressive Dortmund-Ems Canal, which is lined with bicycle and walkways on both sides. For the 30-40 ships that pass through daily, modern twin locks make the increasing volume of freight shipping possible.

1 Dortmund-Ems Canal

River Werse 2

Waterlovers will find ideal spots along the little river named Werse, whose source flows from the Beckum Mountains and into the river Ems. The Werse is a paradise for paddlers and canoeists.

It may be hard to believe but Münster actually has a harbour. Once an important transshipment point for goods, the harbour today is a place of restaurant and a great nightlife scene. Yet it's also the place for the town's creative scene: photographers, architects, designers, painters, sculptors, illustrators, publishers. They all have their studios, offices, and galleries here.

3 Harbour

Rain on the "Prinzipalmarkt"

And finally . . . the matter with the water from above – rain. The papal envoy Fabio Chigi (1548–1611) came to Münster to take part in the negotiations of the Peace of Westphalia (1643–1648). Frustrated after having to put up with the rain, he called Münster literally "homeland of rain". As much as the "Sigh of Chigi" is eagerly quoted, in reality Münster actually receives more hours of sun than the national average and its yearly rainfall is no higher than the national average as well. No rain though can discourage Münster's hardened bicyclists.

Museums, Theatres, Monuments & Sculptures City of Art and Culture

When Münster opened the new LWL Museum of Art and Culture in autumn 2014 whose construction totaled a hefty 48 million Euros, some members of the media joked that Münster has finally arrived in the 20th century.

The response was very positive nationwide thought the Museum deserves the acclaim not only due to its combination of modern architectural elements, particularly the building's pointed design and the so-called "Architecture of Patios" which combines two urban spaces with one another, but also the creation of an immense exhibition area, 7500 m². This is 360 m² more than a football pitch.

The Museum established in 1908 and today managed by the Landschaftsverband Westphalia-Lippe presents 1,200 objects spanning over 1,000 years of art history, from the Middle Ages to today. This includes works from Heinrich Brabender to August Macke, or Lucas Cranach Sen. to Gerhard Richter, all of which is spread out across 51 exhibition rooms.

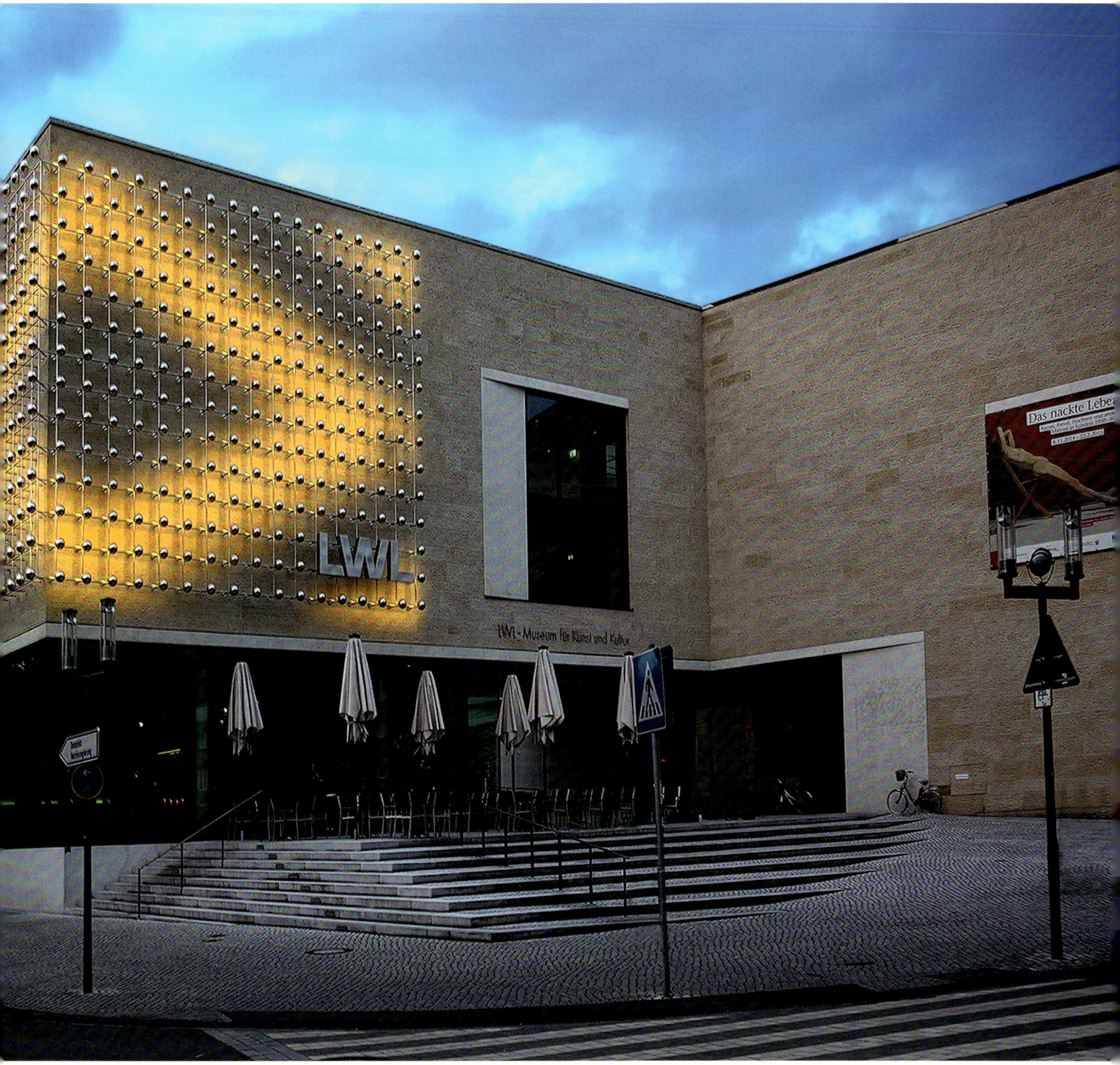
LWL
LWL-Museum für Kunst und Kultur
Das nackte Lebe

The Museum of Art and Culture, as viewed from the Domplatz

Nearby you'll find the Geological Museum, which tells the story of Westphalia's geological development from the Big Bang until today with an exhibition area of 1,300 m^2. There is also the Bible Museum exhibiting the history of the bible from its manuscript beginnings to modern printing, including original pieces such as a Luther Bible from 1545 with a personal inscription from the reformer himself. Not to forget the Archeological Museum, which is filled with art pieces and artisan craftwork of ancient cultures from the Mediterranean and parts of the Middle East. This collection of museums, and the nearby St. Paul's Cathedral Treasury located in the basement of the cathedral called "Domkammer" considered to be one of the greatest in all of Europe, make up the museum quarter.

The Münster Museum of Pablo Picasso Art is unique in Germany. Here, artworks of Picasso, his contemporaries, as well as his artist friends are displayed in alternating exhibitions. From the second storey looking down at the Picassoplatz, you can marvel at a portrait of the artist, compounded of 13,783 cobblestones. The portrait is original in its honouring of the great artist and of the museum dedicated to him.

Picassoplatz from above 1

2 Münster Museum of Pablo Picasso Art

Post mill at the Mühlenhof Open-Air Museum 3

The post mill at the Lake Aa, along with 30 other historical buildings such as a country school and village store, offer an impression of the lives the non-nobility of Münsterland led many years ago. In 1961, the mill "Bockwind Mühle" was relocated from Emsland and brought to the Lake Aa for the opening of the "Mühlenhof Open-Air Museum".

If you're fascinated by lacquerware, there is only one museum in the world exclusively dedicated to this type of art, and it is right here in Münster. The Museum of Lacquer Art, located in the Windhorststraße, is affiliated to the BASF Coatings GmbH, and displays a total of 1,000 pieces of artefacts from Europe, Russia, China, Japan, Korea, as well as from the islamic world.

1 Museum of Lacquer Art

Münster City Museum 2

Behind its Art Deco facade, the Münster City Museum presents Münster's political and cultural history from its beginnings to today through its public collection as well as special exhibitions.

Münster's Municipal Theatre has been described as a "Thunderbolt of Architecture" when opened in 1956. Here are five disciplines under one roof: musical theatre, acting, dance theatre, youth theatre, and symphony orchestra. The theatre integrates the ruins of the manor "Romberger Hof" as a "natural dramatic backdrop". The same spot where the theatre's predecessor, the Lortzing-Theatre, was destroyed during World War II. However, the ruins of the old theatre can still be seen in the inner courtyard of the theatre amongst the trees.

1 Theater Münster – Municipal Theatre

Wolfgang Borchert Theatre at Flechtheim-/Rhenusspeicher 2

Art and culture – the hole raft on a major level! Since fall 2014, Münster is home to one of Germany's oldest private theatres, the "Wolfgang Borchert Theatre". It's located at the harbour in an industrial monument, the renovated Flechtheim/Rhenusspeicher. Here, not only contemporary works are performed, but also more unconventional classical productions.

You can find even more exhibition halls throughout the city such as the Münster Exhibition Hall at the Harbour, the Wewerka Pavillion at the Lake Aa, as well as the additional special houses and vaudevilles of the theatre. However, as impressive as the museum landscape is, there is even more making Münster a city of art and culture: numerous monuments and sculptures expressing a melange of traditional and modern art. On the traditional side there are the stone sculpture of the famous German poet at St. Lamberti Church and the Kiepenkerl-Monument. Münster's more modern sculptures are often purchased by the city during the international exhibition "Sculpture Projects", which takes place every 10 years and displays modern and avant-garde sculptures.

Münster Exhibition Hall at the harbour

Münster has been hosting the Sculpture Projects since 1977 and thereby continues to show its commitment to modern art. During the exhibition, the city landscape is transformed and filled with sculptures and installations from renowned artists and becomes an internationally recognised exhibition space for contemporary art. Art critics praise the exhibition highly and value it even higher than the exhibition "Documenta" in the town Kassel. Though many of the sculpture pieces are temporary, some do indeed become permanent fixtures and, as the Giant Pool Balls of Claes Oldenburg illustrate, are even elevated to landmark status.

Giant Pool Balls

Each of the three giant cement pool balls at the Lake Aa has a diameter of 3.5 m and all of them are positioned as if they were waiting to be struck by a giant billiard cue. The giant pool balls were placed there by the artist Claes Oldenburg within the very first Sculpture Projects in 1977. Interestingly enough, the sculptures faced stiff protests from some citizens, who even attempted to roll them into the Lake Aa. Nowadays though, removing the balls would be unthinkable in the eyes of many Münsterans. The sculpture is hardly ever in its original cement color condition but constantly covered with graffiti or posters. This isn't surprising, since its location on the open grass at the city side of the Lake Aa is a popular spot for pupils and students in the summer who often sunbath and barbeque there.

Cherry Column 1

Another sculpture that has managed to cement itself into the Münster's city landscape is the Cherry Column of Thomas Schütte. In 1987 it was positioned at the "Harsewinkelplatz" and depicts XXL-sized cherries on a pedestal of a column made out of a material common in the city's architectural landscape: sandstone.

Ask yourself, do the two holy figures on the facade of the St. Lamberti Church facing the Prinzipalmarkt appear somehow familiar? You're right! (or wrong!), they're none other than, Goethe and Schiller. The sculptor Anton Rüller (1864–1936) immortalised the German poets on the church facade in 1910. Whereas Goethe's pensive look is easily recognisable, Schiller's appearance is less distinguishable, due to the fact that little is known of Schiller's appearance from his youth today.

2 Goethe, representing the Evangelist Lucas (left)

"Kiepenkerl" Monument at Spiekerhof 3

The Kiepenkerl Monument at the "Spiekerhof", which is actually a replica of the original statue from the Münster sculptor August Schmiemann (1846–1927), shows a travelling trader on his way – a depiction of Münsterland as it once was. The statue shows a man dressed in a linen tunic, scarf, hat, with a walking stick and a basket filled with regional products like eggs, ham, and vegetables. He was not only welcomed into the city because of his products, but also because of his role as bringer of news. What happened to the original? Well, it did indeed survive World War II undamaged. But later it was knocked over and damaged by a British tank while maneuvering.

Only a few kilometers away from the inner city in a little manor named "Rüschhaus" lived and worked Annette von Droste-Hülshof from 1826 to 1846, the most important poet of Westphalia and the best known German poet of the 19th century (1797–1848). Hidden between trees at the "Promenade", she looked out from her peaceful environment out onto the colourful life there.

1 Bust of Annette von Droste-Hülshoff at Kreuzschanze

"Pendelum" 2

"Two Gray Double Mirrors for a Pendulum" by the world-famous painter and sculptor Gerhard Richter (*1932) in the profaned Domenican Church is a new highlight in the art scene of the town. The artwork consists of a Foucault pendulum with a metal sphere weighing 48 kilograms that swings in the centre of the building between four upright, rectangular, mirrored glass panels on a stainless steel cord with a length of 28.75 metres. In this atmosphere of art, science and religion every visitor can get lost in his own thoughts.

The work of the famous English sculptor Henry Moore (1898–1986) is also present in Münster. His bronze sculpture "Large Vertebrae" located in front of the Landesbausparkasse along the street "Himmelreichallee" shows three oversized vertebrae, and offers unique perspectives from various viewpoints since each vertebra is free-standing. The entire piece, including the base, has a size of 72 m^3.

3 Large Vertebrae at LBS

1 100 Arms of Guan-yin

2 ... from below

If you suddenly see 50 arms reaching for the sky mixed with mundane objects such as brooms and hooks, then you have come across the "bottle rack" by the Chinese-French artist Huang Yong Ping (*1954). This sculpture, which was erected as a allusion during the 1997 Sculpture Projects exhibition, is located south of St. Ludgeri Church on the square "Marienplatz" and is a reference to the buddhist goddess "1000 Armed Guanyin". According to the artist, the idea for this sculpture was spawned by the Christ statue in the St. Ludgeri Church, which lost both arms during an air raid in World War II.

There he is, Hermann Landois (1835–1905), grinning to himself at the entrance of the All-Weather Zoo. A true Münsteran through and through, he is the founder of the Westphalian Zoological Garden. It was up to his fellow and contemporary Münsteran, sculptor August Schmiemann (1845–1927), who also designed the Kiepenkerl Monument, to create a sculpture of him. The naturalist Landois, also known by his quirky manner, is depicted with painstaking detail with respect to his typical posture, gestures, and facial expressions. One of his particular jokes is the nesting box in his hat for birds, so that – as Landois himself said – at least the monument will serve some usefulness.

3 Effigy of Landois at the All-Weather Zoo

The waters of the Lake Aa are calm. On the Pardo-Steg, a 40 m long footbridge extending into the Lake Aa with a viewing platform and open pavillion, you'll get the best views of the lake and the city skyline. The installation's title is "Pier" and was constructed by the Cuban artist Jorge Pardo (*1963) during the 1997 Sculpture Projects exhibition.

"Pier" by Jorge Pardo 1

2 The moon in Alabama

As for the area around the train station, light installations give shape to the city's image. For Tobias Rehberger's (*1966) art project called "The Moon in Alabama", he fitted eleven gray telecommunication and traffic signal switchboxes with cartoonish colorful pipes and round illuminating bulbs that embody the moon. The pipes also serve as benches, thereby inviting you to interact with the art pieces.

Flowers, Fruits & Vegetables, Trinkets & Crafts, Ferriswheel & Tunnel of Horror

Market Square in Münster

There's an old saying in Germany: you really get to know a person not at church, but at the market.

Twice a week at the Cathedral Square (Domplatz), the colourful weekly market with over 150 market stalls takes place in a setting that couldn't hardly be any more picturesque and historical. Dominating the ambience and backdrop is St. Paul's Cathedral, with additional views of the steeple of Überwasser Church, the Historical Town Hall, and St. Lamberti Church. On Wednesday and Saturday, the market transforms into a sea of flowers in one area. In another, it's a jungle of fruits and vegetables. There are rows of stands dedicated to fish and meats, breads and cakes, eggs, cheeses, and milk and stands for spices, teas, oils, jewelry, and even doggie treats, too. And of course, there are the potato pancakes, deep fried fish, as well as stew from the field kitchen. The market is not only beloved and visited by Münsterans, but by visitors from surrounding regions as well.

Weekly market at Domplatz

Flea market at the "Promenade"

Grandma's coffee pot, a merry-go-round horse, or old silverware? An opera hat, a bust of Annette von Droste-Hülshoff, or a belling stag in oil? You may find these at the Flea Market, which takes place five times a year along the stretch of the "Promenade" from the City Palace to the Lake Aa. Here you'll find objects that you had no idea you needed. For the bargain hunters and collectors among us, an absolute Eldorado!

Münster's largest fair "Send", with its over 200 stalls, takes place three times a year: Spring, Summer, and Fall – all in front of a gorgeous backdrop: the prince-bishop's City Palace. There is almost everything here belonging to a fair: a gigantic ferris wheel visible from all directions, a nostalgic swing merry-go-round, a tunnel of horror with red-eyed skeletons, and state of the art carnival rides. The numerous stands offer everything from candy floss, pop-corn, and toffee apples, to deep fried fish sand-wiches and hollering raffle sellers.

Ferris wheel at the "Send"

"Send" sword

So that all Münsterans in the inner city know that the fair has returned to Münster, the Send Sword, which is a wooden arm holding a sword upright, is mounted outside of the Historical Town Hall. This signalling of the fair is a tradition dating back to 1578.

Each year during Advent season, Münster's historical centre glimmers and shines not only in the beauty of its historical buildings, but also additionally through the shimmering lights of the five Christmas markets.

1 "Lichtermarkt" at St. Lamberti Church

2 "Giebelhüüskesmarkt" at Überwasser Church

Like pearls on a string they dot the Münster cityscape, each one with its own flair. Mixed in with the atmosphere of warm, almost sepia like lighting, christmas tunes of the street musicians, and richly decorated stands, are the pleasant smells of roasted chestnuts, cinnamon waffles, and mulled wine. Setting not only Münsterans but the visitors (particularly the Dutch) in the jolly pre-Christmas spirit are the many angels and Father Christmases made from all sorts of materials, from metal to gingerbread. There are also countless mangers, wooden toys, and Christmas bulbs and stars. At no other time of year does Münster attract so many tourists than during the Christmas season.

"Halle Münsterland"

Münster is also home to numerous conferences and conventions. The largest conference centre in the region is the "Messe und Congress Centrum Halle Münsterland", which hosts not only international fairs, but also conventions and concerts. With 20,000 m^2 of exhibition space, an 800 m^2 special-event area, as well as 10,000 m^2 for open-air exhibitions, there's plenty of space available.

Highway for Bicycles, Paradise for Joggers, Pedestrians & Rabbits The Promenade

Running along where once the old city walls stood, the "Promenade" and its linden trees wrap around the historical centre and serve as a green belt. It is a 4,8 km long car-free zone.

The "Promenade" is not only a wonderful place to go for a walk as it also serves as the only "bicycle-highway" in Germany. It's so practical. You simply get on the bicycle-highway and shortly before reaching your destination in the inner city, you turn off at the many entrances to the "Promenade". Thanks to this unique infrastructure, you're almost always faster reaching your destination in the inner city on a bike than by car or bus.

Bicyclists on the "Promenade"

Münster was, since the 13th century, defended by a strong fortification system with a moat and a tremendous rampart with guard houses and towers. However, after the Seven Year's War, Franz von Fürstenberg (1729–1810), the prince-bishop's minister and founder of the university, decided to have the fortification system dismantled, in order to build a promenade designed by the baroque architect Johann Conrad Schlaun (1695–1773). Linden trees lining the promenade act as a canopy and form the green ring around the city.

1 The "Promenade" in autumn

Walking along the "Promenade" under the canopy of linden trees through all seasons is an experience to cherish: first a wavy sea of green in the spring, followed by a sweet aroma of linden blossoms in the summer, a burst of warm colours in the autumn, and ending with a thick canopy of bare branches – the "Promenade" is the place of rest and relaxation in the middle of the city.

Snowy paradise in winter 2

There are, however, a few relicts left from the old fortification system. There is the tower "Buddenturm" as the last of once six defensive towers within the inner fortification ring. Then there are the so-called "Wasserbären" (which means water bears) on the street Kleimannstraße as well as on the grounds of the old zoo. The term "Wasserbären", however, has nothing to do with Zoology, but rather is most likely derived from the term "Wasserwehren" (which means water defence). Ten of these formed additional protection in the moats outside of the fortifications.

"Wasserbär"

1 "Buddenturm"

"Zwinger" 2

Lastly, there is the outer ward "Zwinger", left from the old fortifications. Built in 1528, its walls are two metres thick and to this day it appears as a powerful bulwark along the promenade, despite having lost its conical roof in World War II. During this time, the "Zwinger" was used as an execution ground for the Gestapo. Since 1997 though, the ruin was made into an official memorial to all victims of violence.

Manors, Glass & Gables

Balance Between History and Modernity

With the rebuilding of the parlour of Münster, the "Prinzipalmarkt", St. Paul's Cathedral, the City Palace, and the numerous historical buildings, Münster has not only preserved its history, but also at the same time embraced modernity. The city has carefully integrated modern buildings such as the city library, the arcades, as well as the development of the square Stubengasse while creating appealing contrasts with the old.

A few manors are still present in the inner city, bearing witness to the once influential Westphalian aristocracy. These manors served as small castle-like houses, which the aristocracy, particularly in winter, used as their residence. The manors are usually perfectly symmetrical and easily recognisable based on their construction material: sandstone from the nearby Baumberge, red bricks, and many white partitioned windows. This style, which is known as the "Westphalian Symphony", originates from the baroque architect Johann Conrad Schlaun (1695–1773).

MÜNSTER
History and Modernity

"Erbdrostenhof", Salzstraße

Münster's most impressive manor is the three-winged "Erbdrostenhof" located on the street "Salzstraße". Designed and finished by Schlaun in 1758, it rests diagonally on a rather small corner in the inner city. Schlaun managed to create something very majestic out of such constrictions. By using the hypotenuse as the front of the building, he was able to hide the less splendidly decorated outbuildings of the house from view.

The Manor "Heeremanscher Hof" on the street "Königstraße" survived the Second World War mostly unscathed. It's considered one of the major works of the Renaissance in Münster and today houses the Higher Administrative Court and the Constitutional Court of North Rhine-Westfalia.

Manor "Heeremanscher Hof" 1

2 House "Rüschhaus" and its gardens

Münster's gem of late-baroque architecture is undoubtedly the House "Rüschhaus", located outside the city and from 1826–1846 was home to Westphalia's most famous poet Annette von Droste-Hühlshoff (1797–1848). She affectionately referred to this house and here is where she composed many of her works.

House "Rüschhaus", anterior view 3

A typical Münsterland moated castle with a knight's hall is located north of the city. With its over 400 year-old castle cellar and marriage chapel, Wilkinghege Castle now serves as a hotel and restaurant.

1 Wilkinghege Castle

2 District Government façade

History's reflection is found in modernity. In Münster, history is literally found in the modern glass facade of the district government building, giving a reflection of St. Paul's Cathedral.

Big applause for Münster's successful integration of the new into the old! This applies not only to the incorporation of the ruins of the manor "Romberger Hof" with the 1956 modern architecture of the city theatre, but also to the peaceful harmony of old and new in the background – the steeple of St. Lamberti Church and the building of the financial institute "Volksbank".

Patio of the Municipal Theatre 3

Überwasser Church behind the Diocesan Library building 1

Another example of successful contemporary architecture within a historical context is the new Diocesan Library and the Liebfrauen-Überwasserkirche. The library is the central library of the Bishopric of Münster and possesses over 700,000 books and several hundred historical manuscripts, amounting to one of the most comprehensive theological libraries in Germany.

House front at the district "Kreuzviertel" 2

Here is where everyone desires to live – near to the city centre and with special flair: the quarter called "Kreuzviertel". The old buildings of this neighbourhood date back to the turn of the 19th and 20th centuries and are also known for their elaborate facades, high ceilings, and their characteristic floor plan of two upper floors and one attic floor.

3 Front elevations at the district "Kreuzviertel"

"LBS" – "Landesbausparkasse" 1

Like a powerful ship in a harbour, the LBS building, which was designed by the Münster architect Harald Deilmann in the late 60s, sits as if enthroned on the green meadow overlooking the Lake Aa.

2 "LBS" at night

3 "Stubengasse" façade

4 "Stubengasse"

With its off-set arranged levels, the individual buildings of the hotel in the square "Stubengasse" don't appear so dominant. Together with the neighbouring mixed-used building "Hanse Carré", which placed single-family homes with small gardens on top of offices and businesses, the "Stubengasse Development" won the city construction prize in 2010.

Multistorey building "Iduna" 2

A giant under urban heritage conservation: The eleven storey Iduna-Highrise is an office and business building, which was built in the beginning of the 1960s in a precast concrete skeleton construction.

3 "Krameramtshaus" (on the right side)

In 1589, the merchants' guild erected the the building "Krameramtshaus" on the street "Alter Steinweg", adorned with stepped gables, fanned wheels, and a wrought-iron weathervane. It's one of the few buildings in the historical centre, that survived the air raids of World War II relatively unscathed.

Right next door to the Krameramtshaus is the municipal library, which was opened in 1993 and today is one of the most frequented libraries in North Rhine-Westphalia. The library does not only attract book lovers. Its extraordinary architecture is composed of two parts – one of which resembles a ship – that are connected via a bridge on the first floor while sharing the ground floor.

1 Entrance to the Municipal Library

2 Glass dome in the "Münster-Arcades"

A shopping area with roughly 40 stores forms the heart of the "Münster-Arcades", which was finished in 2006. Facing the streets of "Rothenburg" and "Ludgeristraße", the "Münster-Arcades" replicated the archways of the "Prinzipalmarkt" with a modern angular design.

"Münster-Arcades", Ludgeristraße 3

Directly vis-à-vis from the "Münster-Arcades" at the corner of the streets "Rothenburg" and "Königsstraße" is a bank and office building with modern yet gothic-inspired pointed arches on the top floor.

Business house at the corner of "Rothenburg" and "Königsstraße" 1

The office towers of the "LVM", as viewed from Lake Aa 2

3 "LVM" insurance towers

Near the Lake Aa the striking office towers of the LVM insurance company are situated. Made of glass and slanted 63 m into the air, one of them is connected to its 7 m taller adjacent office tower via a glass bridge.

Gaudeamus igitur, Pub Culture & Iconic Pubs Münster's Pub Scene

"An Eldorado for philistines – Cavete Münster!" Cavete is Latin for "take heed". With these words the university student Winfried Weustfeld cautioned in 1958 as he published an article in the university magazine "Semesterspiegel". Today, the warning is still quoted in the menu of "CAVETE", the oldest student pub in the city: "A nirvana on earth! Ade joie de vivre! Gaiety and Humor! You're banished outside of these walls!"

No wonder then, that several years after this proclamation, two students founded the "Academic Pub CAVETE", which is still today popular among students and non-students alike.

Today, numerous pubs have attained cult-status in Münster. "Gaudeamus igitur", meaning "Let us rejoice!" is the motto of the quarter "Kuhviertel", Münster's historical pub neighbourhood with restaurants offering typical Westphalian cuisine, too. In the summer, the neighbourhood becomes one big beer garden, with beer tables and benches from each bar set up outside shoulder to shoulder. You absolutely must try the "Altbierbowle", a popular drink made from dark beer, fruit syrup, and pieces of strawberries or peaches.

JEVER
ZIEGE

1 Sign outside "Cavete"

2 Sign outside "Pinkus Müller"

3 "Altbierbowle"

The "Kuhviertel" has yet another specialty on offer: the dark beer brewery of "Pinkus Müller". At one point Münster had as many as 150 dark beer breweries. However, today stands only one, and that is Pinkus Müller. Dating back to 1816, today the dark beer brewery produces up to 20,000 hectolitres for its 10 tasty hops and malts varieties.

"Blaues Haus" and Münster's tiniest pub "Ziege"

A fleeting visit to this location is not reserved only for former students: the traditional restaurant "Stuhlmacher" right by the Town Hall.

Sign outside "Stuhlmacher" 2

3 "Stuhlmacher"

And so that the pubs in Münster can be easily found, many of them hang their artistic and at times numerous signs above the entrances.

Westphalian hospitality around the "Kiepenkerl" Monument

At one of Münster's most beautiful public spaces, the "Spiekerhof", you'll find three "Kiepenkerle": The first "Kiepenkerl" is the actual monument made by August Schmiemann, that depicts the once "travelling salesman" of Münsterland. The two other "Kiepenkerle" are the restaurants, "Großer Kiepenkerl" and "Kleiner Kiepenkerl", which frame the monument and offer typical rustic homemade Westphalian cuisine.

Harbour

Like Phoenix rising from the ashes, the once destroyed harbour has molted into a nightlife district: cafés, restaurants, pubs, broadcasted football matches, agencies, architect offices, law firms, fitness studios, and a restored grain silo with over thirty ateliers.

During good weather the harbour is quite the open-air event, in which you can either enjoy your long-drink under palm trees as you sink your toes into the sand, or simply enjoy a cold beer on the pier wall. Various restaurants do their part by providing a wide array of options: German, Italian, Latin American, and other international cuisines. And if that wasn't enough: once a year the festival "Hafenfest" takes over Münster's maritime nightlife district during three days and nights. The varied programme with lots of music is one of the highlights in Münster's event calendar.

Pumpernickel, Pancakes & Ham

Classic Münster Cuisine

Münster's cuisine is Westphalian cuisine: simple, rustic, hearty, honest . . . and most of all: delicious. Calorie counting skinny models look elsewhere! Tradtionally established food comes in adapted variants, too.

By listing just a few names of some typical dishes found on many Münsteran menus, you'll see there's nothing short of amazing on offer . . .

"Schlodderkappes"– a dish made from potatoes and white cabbage,

"Potthucke" – a casserole made with grated potatoes and sour cream,

"Blindhuhn" (which means blind hen) – a stew made from white beans, potatoes, pears, and bacon. Strangely enough though, there's no chicken in the stew. The name comes from the idea that even a "blind hen" will find something tasty in the stew.

Let's begin now though with the most famous of Münster's cuisine: pumpernickel, the compact dark brown/black rye whole grain bread with caramelised starch has had a stellar career. Surely, there are some who still compare it to saw dust, but for most it's been rightfully elevated to a kind of national culinary treasure. It's also used as a bottom layer for the so-called "Münsterland Triumvirate": pumpernickel with Westphalian ham and cold beer . . . and best topped with fried egg or finished with Westphalian corn schnapps, or even both.

MÜNSTER's
Cuisine

BRINKHOFF's
PREMIUM No1 PILSENER
KIEPENKERL

1 "Pumpernickel"

"Blindhuhn" 2

3 "Münsterländer Struwen"

But there are pumpernickel gourmet options like pumpernickel cream, pudding, sauce, and brittle. Experts are in disagreement, however, over the origin of the term Pumpernickel. The more entertaining explanation speaks of a Napoleonic soldier, who, after eating the bread, is to have said, that it's only suitable for his horse "Nickel" (c'est bon pour Nickel). A less entertaining explanation has the Latin phrase "bonnum particulum" (good bread) as its source.

And then there's the ham – it's alleged to fill the skies of Westphalia. As a matter of fact, there is a so-called "Westphalian Sky", which is namely the space above an open hearth, where in the older farm houses ham is left to dry. You can still see this today in the quarter "Kuhviertel": e.g. at the restaurant "Pinkus Müller".

An authentic smoked ham from Münsterland has a particularly fine aroma, a light nutty flavor, and it is dry and tender to the taste. The famous German poet Heinrich Heine (1797-1856) himself declared Münsterland in one of his poems to be "the homeland of ham".

The traditional Good Friday dish in Münsterland is the yeast pancake called "Struwen". Though there's no good reason not to enjoy this delicious dish on any other day.

Pancake with bacon 1

One variant of Münsterland pancakes among many has a gold-yellow colour and is made of fried strips of bacon and stewed apples. Other varieties are made of buckwheat and sugar beet syrup.

Then there is the delight of an authentic "Westphalian Töttchen". While considered poor man's food in earlier times due to it being made from the innards of pigs, today it's a Münster specialty and consists of calf's head, heart, and roulette and thereby resembles a ragout fin.

Another delicacy is the so-called "Möppkesbraut" and "Liärberbraut" (which means sausage and liver bread). While "Möppkesbraut" is made from pork, liver, onions, flour, and spices, Liärberbraut is made of blood sausage and whole grains. However, both are not used as spreads, but rather are cut into pieces, fried, and served with "Schmoräppelkes" (fried apple slices) and sugar beet syrup.

2 "Möppkesbraut" and "Liärberbraut"

"Pfefferpotthast" 3

For a very old Westphalian goulash-like stew try the "Pfefferpotthast". Consisting of meat and bread, this stew was once found on many wedding tables. "Pfefferpotthast" is cooked with lots of onions and its base is thickened with old shredded pieces of bread. This dish is commonly served with salted potatoes, red beets, and cucumbers.

And don't forget – no matter what you eat, definitely wash down the local food with a local "schnäpsken": authentic Münsterland corn schnapps!

And finally: The Münsterlander himself

Westphalian stubborn and intelligent?

Münsterlanders are described as rather stubborn and this characteristic can be traced back to their creation myth: Jesus went with the Apostle Peter for a walk through the oak forests, that once surrounded Münster. Peter confessed a liking to the area and asked Jesus, whether he should create a person to populate these lands. Jesus agreed and kicked up the earth with his bare foot and he created a large and strong person from this lump. This person, however, instead of thanking Jesus, jumped up and grunted "Who's been kicking at me?"

Are Münsterlanders really as stubborn as they are portrayed? Of course they may not be everybody's darling straightaway, but as soon as you really get to know them, what may take time, you are friends for life. Well, that's the reason why locals say "You don't really know a Münsterlander until you've eaten a sack of salt together". But after that, indeed!

And what about the intelligence? As a matter of fact Münsterlanders are described as very teachable and intelligent, but this applies to those Münsterlanders with four paws, and this description originates from the dog breed registry. The origins of these four-legged friends can be traced back to Münsterland just as the name suggests. As long ago as the 19th century, hunting dogs were being bred here from medieval hounds.

Would you like to read more about Münster topics in English? We recommend our English books to you. Please visit our online-shop (www.muenstermitte-medienverlag.de) or simply ask Münster's booksellers:

Etzkorn, Münster & Countryside – Welcome

Peter, Münster-Souvenirs

Rammes, Münsterland – The little Cookbook from Town & Country

Photo credits:
Page 9 picture 2: Presseamt Münster/Münsterview; page 17 picture 1: Presseamt Münster/Münsterview; page 21 picture 2: Helmut Peter Etzkorn, Münster, page 37 picture 1: Allwetterzoo Münster; and all the rest oft them: Gösta Clemens Peter, Münster.

Imprint:

Münster at its Best – The Sightseeing Book
2nd Edition

www.muenstermitte-medienverlag.de

Setting & Layout: Stefanie Meyer, Münster
Printed in Germany: Bitter & Loose GmbH, Greven

ISBN: 978-3-943557-52-7